SAXOPHONE BLUE

MICHAEL CALVELLO

DATE DUE

8 2010

SAXOPHONE BLUE

MICHAEL CALVELLO

Ithuriel's Spear

San Francisco

ACKNOWLEDGMENT

Grateful acknowledgment is made to the following magazines where some of these poems have appeared: Ally 81, American Pen, American Scholar, Blue Unicorn, Colorado-North Review, Gazebo, Haight-Ashbury Literary Journal, Hyperion, Icarus, Langston Hughes Review, Many Mountains Moving, Mikrokosmos, Minotaur, Poetry U.S.A., Silver Wings, The Acorn, The Altadena Review, & The New Moon Review.

Cover and book design by Plainfeather Printworks.

Front cover painting "longest day of the year, twilight" by Gage Opdenbrouw, at www.engageingart.com.
Back cover photo by author.

ISBN 978-0-9793390-4-2

Library of Congress Control Number: 2009932973

Ithuriel's Spear is a fiscally sponsored project of Intersection for the Arts, San Francisco.

www.ithuriel.com

CONTENTS

TO KNOW TIME

San Francisco Dream

*for Harvey Milk and George Moscone**

"I am just a dreamer but you are just a dream."
—Neil Young

I

left Wichita, 1978
coming back to San Francisco

walking near City Hall
I heard the shots that killed
Moscone and Harvey Milk

loud bangs
that scattered the pigeons
bleeding and blurred

the fog
down Twin Peaks
whipping through Castro Valley

*George Moscone, Mayor of San Francisco
Harvey Milk, the first gay SF Supervisor

II

sky and houses
a back yard morning

the eucalyptus
curves in wind
tapered leaf in sun light

somewhere
someone is burning eucalyptus
sweet smoke for these men

III

the wind off Lake Merced
Lake Merced is shrinking
going straight down into itself

the ducks swim
the rain's a sheet of gray

a column of wind
moves across the lake
sends ripples wider

IV

in the early Fifties
living on the south side of Bernal Heights
climbed to the top
before it was bulldozed
for a siren

before they chopped off
another piece of earth

they hid the gash with evergreens
pines and cypresses
that caught the fog

one last time
I stood on Bernal Heights
looked south
at the huge San Bruno Mountains

half hidden in fog
driven by a strong west wind
going in and out of shadows

black fog on the mountain
like the back of an animal
shapes changing their shapes

                    V

red span
Golden Gate Bridge
entrance to the north
an earth red

these Marin hills rise toward Tamalpais

Mount Tamalpais
I want to dream them back again

men running the open fields of Castro Valley

to know time

for Jack Kerouac

watching
the blue twilight
turning black

driving across America
dark brown
earth-road

your fingers grip the wheel
feel the wanderer's void

up black mountain
you see
the bones of your fathers
on the dark slopes

crawling green
from the furrows
eating the earth

mountain cloud air
red boxcar red engine
rumbling Buddha eyes

red mouth red wine
your black curls of hair

Jack, these are your eucalyptus
in San Francisco

glint of sun
on pointed leaves

a man
walking through
his light

grows from the shadows
slides over the leaves

Eucalyptus Poem

for Lew Welch

"Barbara, think what'd happen if
Van Gogh'd ever seen eucalyptus trees."
                                    L.W.

Lew, he would have them swirling
in gray fog along El Camino
he would have them covering
the earth with seeds
brown buttons
marked on one side
a four-pointed star

he would paint their leaves slender
tapered on both ends
glittering in the sun

he would have them touched with light
the wind moving through them
swaying above St. Mary's Park

he would paint the tallest eucalyptus
in a line of black green
wind-breaker for artichoke farms

and Lew, in moonlight
Van Gogh would make them mother-of-pearl
around the cross on Mount Davidson

The Light above the Cross
on Mount Davidson

read in the newspaper
there was a strange light
above Mt. Davidson

they said it could have been
Mars or Venus
both of them
the closest to earth now
and not again
for thousands of years

but nothing was for sure
only that there was a strange light
over Mt. Davidson

the highest point of these
San Francisco hills

"golden eternity"

From the novel *Dharma Bums,*
Jack Kerouac

another windy afternoon
the white sun moves in and out
of fog

sitting on top of Holly Park
a circle of green
up high in San Francisco

the view of Twin Peaks
Mount Davidson
and the blue bay

tone of grey
clouds moving in from the Pacific

eucalyptus and pine
creak in the wind

near your face
grass blades and dandelions
flower in the open field

in the east
the bay stretches across the earth

in a blue haze
Mount Diablo
a huge pyramid shape

Mount Diablo
rock face
waiting to be named

Maya Fog

our flesh is real
sun burnt in summer
and sure to be cold
white marble sheets in winter
a long dark solstice

and yet
the flesh is real
soft and blue veined

a butterfly dance
to the fog

windy eucalyptus hill
of San Francisco

Mission Valley Mythos

a summer
in the fog of San Francisco
warm early valley
in the mission sun

I remember
you were full
in the hot harvest

sticky brown resin female
you are always stronger
on my caveman palm

dark red rose and peeling leaves
in the eucalyptus hilly
San Francisco fog

tell me,
what kind of festivities,
what kind of magic, dancing races
of this April wind from Twin Peaks
did those Mission brown Indians

play in the young corn
slopes of Castro Valley

she would love me
like a star
delicately lights the dark spaces
and calls no name

as you pass by
the sudden glance
irrevocable as dawn

is that a flute in your hands
for the breath to cover us in music
the wind of our bodies

falling apart in Eros

City, San Francisco

"the basic tones of existence"
                Jack Kerouac

black grays
fog on the San Bruno Mountains
late afternoon
play of children
shadows thinning over eucalyptus

almost at the winter solstice
a child sees the few flowers

daisy
buttercup under her chin
to see the yellow glow

the fog slides over hilly streets
the yellow sun
changes to gray
light around the edges

where is the angel in this room
this city
that beats inside your heart

Zen Blues

"I've got new eyes.
 Everything looks far away."
                    Bob Dylan

the mind begins
to see distances

grey clouds
settle on the hills

the path to the summit
is lost in mist

lovers recede
inside their separate rooms

their passion
spreads out over the fields
darkening the edges of twilight

Images with Neruda

textured light
criss-crossing your room
shape of solitude

blue light on the sea
a bell faintly ringing disappears
the sound of waves returns

a blue infinity
in a clear sky

on a cloudy day
you're closer to trees and earth
the clouds keep the distance away

without the sun
the clouds have no color

purple, violet,
turn into grey

stars in their galaxies
a man under the pine

Diego Rivera Mural Song
Pan-American Unity

1

the long body of the snake Quetzalcoatl
white fangs coming at you
blue yellow
red plumes

2

the brown Indians smell the earth
one of them wants to fly
he stands with yellow paper wings

Indians are making jewelry
making a fire
deer-headed Indians
weavers musicians
and the huge brown hand
Latino hand earth hand
with four turquoise-blue stars
raised to you

3

Indians watching Washington
America beginning to form
and the Indians dying
under silver bayonets, bullets
black cannons

World Wars
the steel machine has steel fangs
and part of a brown hand

half-flesh, half-robot
the face is white-grey, brown
steel fangs facing you

barb wire Nazi wrist
holds a dagger
the American flag is draped over an arm
holds the dagger away

a dead body over barb wire
sick yellow insect man
tear gas man over barb wire

4

all of us sitting among steel machines
but there is
man and woman
they hold thin roots
a tree of life
between them

she wears a white dress
in a blue shirt
blue jeans

and Diego
almost lost in all of this

an artist
painting a misty sailboat

SAXOPHONE BLUE

Saxophone Blue

Ben Webster notes
on this Sunday night

the last two candles
giving a dim
gold light

like Ben's softness
his moody wandering
watercolor sounds
whispering

muffled, woody
reeds in the wind

The Musician

for my father

his clarinet
was there for me
in the late forties

I remember
a chromatic run
rising and falling

on Sunday afternoons
all the way
through the fifties

he would practice for hours
in the bedroom on Gates Street
lost in a sliding sound

the blues
felt so good
in his head

Flamenco Sketches

sounds opening
to Coltrane's music

his saxophone this time
a meeting of sun and leaves
transparency, light-veined

Coltrane, the poem is coming down to you

singing beyond scales
black bird
riding on top of time

Poem Jazz Hawaii

to Moon

music
through the rooms
of rented houses

he blows his horn
to a blue sky
his light touch
moves up and down

comes 'round
the corners of the wind

soft jazz
sweet jasmine
in night air

his music
with the night coming on

soft and woven
space between the sounds

moon jazz
mother-of-pearl night

his breath
making the air come through
giving the music

Louis Armstrong Plays for His Wife in Giza, 1961

in the photograph
he is standing in a black suit
holds his trumpet up high
at the white sky

his wife watches him
she is smiling

the Sphinx head
is huge, jagged

Louis' face
and the face of the Sphinx
are the same face
the Pyramid towers
above all of them

Louis, what were you playing?
was it a melody from a song
a pure riff
of one or two long notes
circling in the Egyptian air

Riff for Charlie Parker

"I could hear it sometimes
  but I couldn't play it."
                    Charlie Parker

your breath
coming from your belly
your fingers
running the keys

saxophone flying
eyes closed
inside the sounds

black jazz nights
coming from your head
the changes
above the melody

meandering
blue chords
deep from your body

Charlie, I hear you
in the rain falling
on purple ti-leaves

in the waves
from the wind
trailing into mist

Coleman Hawkins

you must be
one of Coltrane's fathers
the way you stand
between swing and the zen void

playing "Picasso"
cubist sounds darken
modulations
leave the melody

on the edges
the changes
into slow "La Rosita"
with another tenor man
Ben Webster

you blend your sounds
both saxophones
harmonizing into one

Telephoning after Coltrane

for my father

two months before he died
he called in the afternoon
his voice excited
sounding so young for 89 years

"that's how I want to play," he said,
"like Coltrane"
his saxophone flowing in our heads
deep feelings, fingers searching
"that's how I want to play," he said
in a happy tone
before he started getting hoarse
before the thyroid cancer
silenced everything

except being with Coltrane's
sound of rushing light
from here on in

CAIRO DREAM

Cairo Dream

the color
an ancient gold
in candle light

studying the Egyptian Tarot
in an orange tent
in Amsterdam

the black
triangular design
on the face of the cards

the human figures
the woman's hand
in the mouth of the lion

her soft body
swaying like a tree

these branches of the road
the legs
a sling-shot V

two women
tapping on your shoulder
cawing of birds

Egyptian Man

in an old railroad flat
on Dolores Street
standing in front
of the mirror
reflections of the dark
Berkeley hills

black and red shadows
circle an older man
staring back at me

through my eyes
green-brown veins of leaves
criss-crossing me

an ash-grey skull
our faces
I hold a candle and stare

his head is covered
in dark cloth

when I relax my eyes
a deep red appears
then fades away

becoming the light
on the Berkeley hills

a yellow sun
rising dawn
over Mount Diablo

Egyptian Tree Prayer

thick oak of Eden
slender sycamore
in the apple sun

the snake
slides in the dark leaves glides
in the cool leaves,
tongue in and out
in the dark apple sun

in that thick black oak
in Eden,
when she came,
green veined,
emerald eyes,
lady of the green tree
give me roots
and trunk feet winding yours,
running in the shadows
of the night green field

for I hear the cry of Anubis man
hear his fingers
balancing the stones

in the cave
of the mountain

Song for Nijinsky

your cubist body
your palms turned upward
ankles of a bird
you danced Debussy's
The Afternoon of a Faun

arms bent
a string of leather
on your thick neck

you are kneeling, Nijinsky
the Egyptian line of your body
high cheekbones
animal man

God pulling you open to dance

Dusty Foot

"a wayfarer, a traveler, applied to Death
personified"

(O.E.D.)

looking through time-tables
of train stations
he wonders when he will leave

his dust settles on all things

goes into corners
a powdery
white gray
on table tops
on books
dust in front
on the edge of wooden space

particles from the sky
breathing in the dust
he moves his fingers through it

dust on the window sill
"the soul, that dwells within your dust"
 somewhere Dante said

he walks
leaving a trace of dust
lightly on your face

at a vaudeville show
three musicians
a piano, tin drum
tambourine

a painted scene
brown hills
with fuzzy trees

and Dusty Foot comes zig-
zagging
across the stage

a tall man
with an angular face

a staccato tapping
to his crazy dance

his black fedora
tilted to the side
covered in dust

smears of it
on his black coat and shoes

gray dust falling
like pollen
over his triangular form

Mango Darkness

Mango Darkness

not the sweet fruit
but the shadows
these mango trees
make under the sun

a sudden wind
two brown pheasants
fly into the leaves

moving closer in the rain
to the center of the tree

the space inside
black green

knowing this place
mirror of Wailuku River
green river
boulders bleached gray
the mouth
water smooth

night fishing on Keawe Bridge
the fishermen talk
watch the lines of their poles

black river of broken light
where the fishermen stare

today I saw one
snap the pole
over his shoulder
his body one quick arc

Onekahakaha Beach Park

by the outdoor shower
she holds her child
waiting peacefully
in her arms

she barely turns the water on
flicks her fingers
over him

he blinks his eyes
in sunlight
both of them laughing

Gemini Song

for my son, Michael

1

on a foggy June
you were born

your small form
your purple face
bruised cheekbones
pulled out with forceps

you began squinting
in a San Francisco morning

in fog
the grey cross
on Mount Davidson

eucalyptus
swaying on the hills

and the earth your Mother
still holding you

2

years later
in Hawaii
you were lost on the volcano
walking the lava roads
with friends somewhere

looking for you
the red earth
black lava rock
smoldering crust

waiting all afternoon
for you to come back
facing the ridge
with the dark coming on

the black ridge almost gone
shadows moving over the ground

crying for you
hiking the pig trails
with the Hawaiians

walking all night with flashlights
the strong sulfur smell
from the eruption
lava breaking
brittle glass flakes
chips of gray rock

where is Madame Pele*
taking you?
did you drop inside her lava tube
a bolt of fire
shooting a tunnel
through rock to the sea

all night walking
and the hope dying
with the grey Hawaiian dawn

over the rim's edge
the O'hia trees
blackened from the heat
twisted shapes
the fresh lava
breaking and smoking

looking for the lost son
on the red earth

*Hawaiian Fire Goddess of the Volcano

3

in the morning
one last ride
with the park ranger
in the green jeep

up ahead
your blue shirt
on the lava rock

and still wandering the open fields
calling your name

and suddenly
your tiny voice

your small form waving

A New Child

A New Child

who is it
keeping me
in desire
burning the flesh away
in a solitary vision

O let the stars
be the irises in our eyes

who is it
keeping me
in a steady fear

O bless the old men
fondling their withering seed
and all old women
keeping the memory
in their thighs alive

a new child
staring in wonder
at the circling stars

The Small Boy

I was not the small boy
sitting near wrinkled-lipped women
in drab coats
with mouths of faiths
echoing in a foreign mumbling
of some church
where candles flickered
the golden dance
under leg stumps on the bloody cross.

No—I was not the small boy.
I have been told by others.

I was not the boy
who got the dry kiss
from ancient parentage
nor the warmth of ritual handshake
nor the periodic pat on the head.

But here now
I—thrown in moldy trust
cascading down jumbled years
the grey at temples
the after-dinner drink with smile
wearing tight white collars
and pastel ties
and squatting in a patch
of yellow weeds
directionless and no guide

not even a priest I can reason with

Images, Winter and Fall

sitting on the vanity bench
watching falling snow
discarded Christmas trees
the dying of 1943
the scrap drive for Victory
and burning Poland

so I ask my mother
can Superman really fly?
while Mrs. Mahoney rocked in her chair
her shawl hugging freckled hands
when the siren starts

it was hard
to go to sleep
in black-outs

though coming back from Christ
I remember the ritual
of roaming on Halloween
all over San Francisco

to come home spreading a paper bag
red suckers popcorn
wax dolls filled with kool-aid

I was always a tramp
with a red-checkered handkerchief
on a stick
stuffed with rags--
words, image
of my father burning
a cork over the gas flame
the smell scraping skin

he gave me his old man's beard
both of us
with blackened faces

Through Dark St. Kevin's

I remember the walk
through dark St. Kevin's
an altar boy passing
the baptism vestibule—
his feet echoing
up the center aisle
of marriage and deaths,
mosaic inscriptions
of a Thursday night holy hour

Rheumatic under white and gold vestments,
Father Guerin waits
in the quiet sacristy,
waits for me
to click open
the metal communion rail latch
and genuflect beneath
the tabernacle candle
burning in red glass

And in the room
across from his,
the service begins—
holding a round black charcoal,
I light the edges
with a thick kitchen match,
then with one finger,
I level the small golden spoon of incense
for the benediction of innocence
in the closed vestry

'Son. Are you ready?'
his slow voice asks
across the dark space
between our rooms
in back of the altar

There, the electric box hangs on the wall—
so, in answer,
I switch on all the lights
with my ten fingers,
the levers snapping all at once
for the ten or twelve people
scattered in wooden pews

And under the bulbed chandeliers,
we sit on a brown mahogany bench
where he reads from a yellow book
until it is time
to move to the altar again.

He steps above me,
raising stiffening arms
to begin his prayer.
I kneel on the first step of red carpet
and sprinkle incense
on the burning charcoal—
the smoke grey-sweet
rises when he turns
and shows the Blessed Sacrament,
its metal strips
and colored stones
swinging in his hands—
and looking down
he nods his head at me

so I ring the small gold bell
in answer again.

Now the old priest is dead.
And I, too, have left
that ghost of an altar boy

running down
towards Father Guerin
sitting in the dark
his body stiffening
as I helped him
in and out of his garments

Was it a naïve smoke I burnt?
And the ringing bell
in supplication—
was it a sound
to mock now
or that mocks me?
That demands a dichotomy of seasons
a polarity of spring
and the new snow—
demands this poem
of words falling
to some order

Outside of St. Kevin's
wind is moving
through that dark holy hour,
and I move, have to,
in spite
of myself

Nacimiento

show me your light*
stranger out there
wandering in darkness
through warring cities
before your birth

over the mantle
leaf-shaped
lights dimming New York City
1944 blackout
the sirens wailing

a child then
wrapped inside
sheets and blankets
you held yourself in

staring at the ceiling
animal shapes
moved over the walls

and over your ears
the sheet kept the cold away
the muffled voices in other rooms

*words told to a young Salvadoran
woman by a *Bruja,* a witch, when
danger is near.

black furrows over the earth
bones of soldiers
field pock-marked by bombs

you slept
curled in a ball

show me your light
young child out there
falling from your Mother

falling through space
through warring cities
before your birth

Once I Rang the Bell

once I rang the bell at St. Kevin's
for an early morning mass
on the south side of Bernal Heights
San Francisco, 1952

I'd run down Gates Street to Cortland Avenue
up the stairs above the choir room
to the bell tower

I pulled the rope hard
my whole body
holding on and swinging

And the bell began to gong above me
soft, then hard
swinging me in the air

Poem for Tony

the words were Langston Hughes
and when you happened
to read them

your seven year old spirit
yelled "the moon is naked"
with laughter and surprise

and your brown eyes
for the first time
saw a naked moon

The Walk

I

this maize October
warm sun
brown scattered leaves
maples and poplars

the crippled old man
drags his limp foot
up the hill

the brown leaves
become dust

in the corners
the houses sleep

II

the old man
has his cane
moving snail-like
his heavy body
dragging one foot sideways
up the hill

I walk towards him
his face is loose and tired
grey as the sidewalk
on which we move

we smile and pass
one another
the same man

slowing down the heart
and the memories

knowing that we are one man walking
this land of bare trees

The Pine Tree

you have no roots
but your feet
walking over
this spring earth

the snow melting
the green moss coming back
the yellow weeds and grass

it is twilight
around your body
your soft indistinct face
in a last light
against the window
before the dark

becomes clear
for one
brief moment of clarity
clear as the wind
through the massive pine
in the open field

you have no roots
no native town to wander in
no land to own
to plant a sunflower in

it is our arms and legs that cling
this ancient pine that touches
and owns the land

Sun

after time
the sun
is leaving the trees
birch and fir stand in the snow
the land is endless and beautiful

stars come
in a deepening sky
the twilight ends
in grey light

is this a song about the sun?
the child asks
where does the sun go

that this sun darkens
this raisin of skin
dried in the wisdom of lizards

that this burnt light on water
this fire
forever upon the breasts of her mountain

bearing the snow to the green ground

The Rose

"The man who said, for the first time,
'I see the rose,' said nothing, but
 the man who said for the first time,
'The rose sees me uttered a very
 wonderful truth."

                          Dylan Thomas
                          Letter, Dec. 25, 1933

if all flowers see us
these redwoods
near Pescadero Road
standing in mist
must know our names
the violence we bear
the smell of sap and blood
mixing in the air

in the delicate seed, Dylan,
sprouting in your hands
blue-veined

you hold a rose
seeing through her eyes

Aurora,
Goddess of the Dawn,
Daughter of Hyperion

"after 1790 auroras became infrequent but
since 1825 they have been on the
increase"

mother of stars
my face keeps turning to the east
mother of stars
of the morning and evening breeze

remembering
a warm spring morning in May
we sat in the library
discussing the Northern Lights

Aurora Borealis
the birth in the storm of the sun
you said particles of light
cascading over the dark blue rolling earth

shapes of ivory light
moving in the dark sky

and underneath
we are dumbfounded
in our science
in the madness of our souls

Aurora Borealis woman of dawn
brings the wind as the breath
in the mouth of your love

flush of scarlet
the beginning light in everything

the first morning
when your lover turns to you
becomes wet and open

Aurora Aurora
the snake curving of her light
the luminous aura

along a beach at morning
the breaking of the dawn

DUENDE

Duende

"Whatever has black sounds,
   has duende."
                              Manuel Torres

the gray edges of the sea
Lorca's raw song
from the throat
of Pastora Pavon
Andalusian singer
"the girl with the combs"

her black sounds
shuddering in her belly
shuddering in her loins
her skin falls
inside her smooth bones

the wind carries the sand
the blood caries the song
her orange mouth
opens the folds of her death

Pastora Pavon
what line did you carve
in the palm of your hand?

your fingers cross
the sides of your face
blue scarlet rose
in your black hair
the wound that never closes

Andalusia Andalusia
your wind
shapes the fall of the sand

Book Man

for M.C. III

barely knowing the man who died
who left behind
his books
on the garage floor
in zig-zag rows
for you to look through

his wife and son stand motionless
watch the books
fill the trunk of the car
smile and say good-bye

Book Man, what book
is there to hold
in these silent hands?

The I Ching

he didn't want to hear about the hexagrams
or of the coins falling
to broken and solid lines
thrown 6 times

he didn't want to see
the image of Standstill
no movement
until the Arousing
until changing lines of shock and thunder

and a man would come
moving light
across the sky

The Photograph

Einstein,
your eyes are deeper than space
sadder than endings
crying in a sky of blood
raining a gray rain
atom bomb
you tried to stop

Einstein, you left
down a hallway of sand
black seaweed, shells,
bits of wood

and no time now
only a humming sound

each wave a galaxy
each sun a heart

The Mountain

for Lew Welch

you walked away
somewhere in the Sierra
making one last path
through the wilderness
up to where you stayed
until you gave your breath
to the place around you

brown rocks
dry earth
your head on the earth
the blood beating in your ears

Baudelaire

in the grey
cold stillness
the blank sky

the snow
melts and freezes
the last white day of February

bluejay, where have you gone?
blue could fill this day

with the smell of wild bird
inside her hair

Hearing Sandy Bull Play
Manha de Carnival

I see age
all around me
my father
a darkness growing
darker my mother
around our eyes
an ancient sadness
in our closet universe

please look in my eyes
and touch me
deep in the place
of my spinning bone

Totem Music

for my father

they carried you out of the
bedroom
wrapped in a white body bag

they held you upright
strapped on a gurney
like a curled flag
so that you would fit
inside the elevator

and as you went by
I remember the music you played

your clarinet
the totem of your family

Autumn Fragments

I

death you are out there
smelling the dark
winding sheet
a hard leathery face
walnut-sunken eyes
a dry raisin mouth
kissing the stars of Egypt

death you are
the old man's
black dog
wandering hastily
among the stones and caves
while the wind
separates the river
swells the rich earth
for the coming of the leaves
that fall in place of flowers

II

walking past the massive
red brick hospital
dark figures
enter the room
gathering around
the dumbfounded eyes
stare for a last time
on the immaculate bed
a laced pillow
with purple flowers
of the old father's daydream

in twilight
the rising moon
the swirling circles of birds

Tree-Branch Man:
Winnebago Trickster Myth

for Gary Snyder

old Coyote sly
in the eye
on one side
of the river
waving all afternoon
and night—
waving eagle feathers
at tree-branch man
pointing at the sky

Up the Mountain

for Caitha

be way up high
lovely dancer
in a thinner air

a vision of cold water
a heady dizzy feeling—
I watch the mountain birds
playing in the snow
calling way up high
to a colder vision
a colder air

our guide is waving us on—
he is beating his drum
he is throwing black crow feathers
in the frozen air
and smiling back at us
and singing

be way up high
spirit man
in a thinner air

way up high

for Jack Kerouac

sweet moment of eternity
on Desolation Mountain
above the clouds

just far enough away
from old man death
sad blue jazz

sweet wine
the belly's dark road
where the mountain bird sings clear

in the late sixties
L.S.D. on vitamin C
tabs you had
years ago

taking the trip alone
for the first time
inside your crazy mind

walking down the hallway on Dolores Street
a railroad flat
where the rooms
were off to the side
of the long hall

where you walked
through red and blue
bands of colors
the energy tasting thick in the throat

and when you walked to the mirror
saw your skeleton face
staring from someone else's eyes

89 years old
and trying to stop it from
spreading
he sits in the radiation room
waiting with thyroid cancer

his throat is marked
inked on his neck
in blue horizontal lines

he leans forward
over his cane
he never wanted to use

sitting
in a stillness
where no one has ever gone

The Painter on His Way to Work, 1888

with a brown back over his shoulders
one hand holds a bucket
the other hand carries an easel

behind him
gold wheat fields
tall and ready for harvest

under an intense sun
he wears a straw hat
his face looks at you

walking down the road
his black shadow
follows along

Lemon-Yellow, Prussian Blue

"They are only to be found in Delacroix, who had a passion for the two colors which are most condemned, lemon-yellow and Prussian blue. I think he did superb things with them."

Vincent Van Gogh

your red hair
Vincent
and the yellow sun
pouring down on you

the red wind
Vincent
tree-limbs
trailing vines
her red thighs
burning into you

Vincent
at dusk
the sower is black-green
is scattering seed

he holds the small plant-flower
near his face
the sun explodes across half the sky
the tree curves in the air

her orange leaves
her cold brown edges
her fields move in you

Vincent
it is your bluest blue
but the blue night changed
the young child's mark
on the white page

you stand
near the black cypress
the starry summer air
and she is the body
you have given her

by the strokes of your hand
and the collapse
of your deep
magenta heart

Old Man in Sorrow, 1890 (On the Threshold of Eternity)

he sits on a wooden chair
burying his face in his fists
leans over
in a dark blue vest
with feet pressed
against the floor

he is bald
except for white strands
over his ears
and down the back of his head

stooped over
on the edge of his chair
there is a small fire near him

and no one knows the grieving
inside his dark hands

Two Lovers, 1888

they walk away
down a brown road
just the back of them

he wears a yellow straw hat
she's dressed in a deep red
skirt and shawl

her arm is around his shoulder
one of his legs is close to her body
she leans into him

and all you know
is that they are walking

between green fields
in the same direction

Self-Portrait, 1887

the words of his face
green eyes staring
so intense

red beard red hair
clipped short

his eyes inside
a deep space

black crows over the road
wheatfield and sky
color in moving light

Vincent, the prism
of your being
gone to the other side

La Nueva Ser

though you can see the shapes of objects
you still don't know
why you are here

surely the changes
in your face
begin to see
the resemblances

ancient markings
grid lines
texture of light through trees

once you were left alone inside a cave
to watch the sky darken
staring at stars

and the sun was the day's light
though it didn't have a name

for the warmth of her
on this green
watery planet

for the silver disc of her
motionless
in the silent air

INDEX